DISASTERS
PEOPLE IN PERIL

FIERY VOLCANO
THE ERUPTION OF MOUNT ST. HELENS

Carmen Bredeson

Enslow Publishers, Inc.
40 Industrial Road
Box 398
Berkeley Heights, NJ 07922
USA

http://www.enslow.com

Original edition published as *Mount St. Helens Volcano: Violent Eruption* in 2001.

Library of Congress Cataloging-in-Publication Data

Bredeson, Carmen.
    Fiery volcano : the eruption of Mount St. Helens / Carmen Bredeson.
      p. cm. — (Disasters—people in peril)
    Includes bibliographical references and index.
    Summary: "Examines the 1980 eruption of Mount St. Helens volcano, including the cause of the eruption, its impact on
      surrounding environments, and stories from survivors"—Provided by publisher.
    ISBN 978-0-7660-4015-1
    1. Saint Helens, Mount (Wash.)—Eruption, 1980—Juvenile literature. 2. Volcanoes—Washington (State)—Juvenile
    literature. I. Title.
    QE523.S23B737 2012
    551.2109797'84—dc23
                       2011037673
Future editions:
Paperback ISBN 978-1-4644-0108-4
ePUB ISBN 978-1-4645-1015-1
PDF ISBN 978-1-4646-1015-8

Printed in the United States of America

032012 Lake Book Manufacturing, Inc., Melrose Park, IL

10 9 8 7 6 5 4 3 2 1

To Our Readers: We have done our best to make sure all Internet addresses in this book were active and appropriate when we went to press. However, the author and the publisher have no control over and assume no liability for the material available on those Internet sites or on other Web sites they may link to. Any comments or suggestions can be sent by e-mail to comments@enslow.com or to the address on the back cover.

♻ Enslow Publishers, Inc., is committed to printing our books on recycled paper. The paper in every book contains 10% to 30% post-consumer waste (PCW). The cover board on the outside of each book contains 100% PCW. Our goal is to do our part to help young people and the environment too!

Illustration Credits: AP Images, pp. 25, 28, 34; AP Images / Austin Post, p. 21; AP Images / Elaine Thompson, p. 42; AP Images / Gary Stewart, p. 31; AP Images / George Wedding, p. 27; AP Images / Harry Glicken, pp. 8, 19; AP Images / Jack Smith, pp. 1, 4; AP Images / Mike Cash, p. 22; AP Images / Sherry Bockwinkel, p. 33; AP Images / Ted S. Warren, pp. 37, 39, 41; Enslow Publishers, Inc., p. 13; J. Rosenbaum / U.S. Geological Survey, p. 17; © North Wind Picture Archives / Alamy, p. 11; U.S. Geological Survey, pp. 7, 14.

Cover Illustration: AP Images / Jack Smith (Mount St. Helens erupting, July 22, 1980).

CONTENTS

THE GIANT ROARS

IN THE SPRING OF 1980, Harry Truman got hundreds of letters from schoolchildren. They begged the old man to leave his home in the state of Washington. Many newspaper articles and television programs had featured the stubborn eighty-three year old. Harry Truman's name was easy to remember because a former president of the United States had the same name. Students were worried about Truman. Just five miles away from his lodge on the edge of Spirit Lake, Mount St. Helens, a volcanic mountain, towered over the landscape.

There had not been an eruption at Mount St. Helens since 1857. Then, on March 20, 1980, a strong earthquake shook the sleeping giant awake. During the next few weeks, hundreds of small earthquakes rocked the 9,677-foot-high mountain. Several times ash and steam escaped from the volcano and blasted into the sky.

Even more ominous than the steam and ash was the bulge that kept growing on the north face of the peak. Pressure building up inside the volcano was pushing out part of the mountain. By the middle of May, the bulge was the size of a football field and stuck out three hundred feet. United States Geological Survey (USGS) geologist David Johnston said, "This mountain is a powder keg, and the fuse is lit, but we don't know how long the fuse is."[1]

Because the volcano might erupt at any moment, members of local and state law enforcement agencies were evacuating people from the "red zone," roughly a twelve-mile area around Mount St. Helens. When officials arrived at Harry Truman's house, the old man refused to leave. "If I got out of here, I wouldn't live a day, not a day. I talk to the mountain, the mountain talks to me," he explained.[2] For more than fifty years, Truman had lived on the banks of Spirit Lake. He planned to stay right where he was, at home with his sixteen cats.

Sheriff's deputies were also having a hard time keeping sightseers away from the mountain. The blasts of ash and steam were fun to watch. The huge bulge on the north face of the peak did not seem to scare people, either. There was almost a holiday mood around the mountain during the spring months of 1980. Families brought picnic lunches to nearby lookout points, sat on blankets, and waited to see what would happen next. Hikers went around roadblocks and up winding paths to get a better look at the volcano. Photographers tried to get a little closer to take pictures of the incredible bulge.

By Saturday, May 17, 1980, the mountain had settled down a little. Many of those who had been evacuated from the red zone wanted to check on their houses and pick up extra clothes. Deputies agreed to let

Two geologists take photographs of the volcano's north side prior to the eruption on May 1, 1980. A huge bulge of steam and ash continued to grow on the north face of the peak. By mid-May, the bulge stuck out three hundred feet.

them visit their homes, but only long enough to collect some of their belongings. After returning to safe areas Saturday afternoon, residents were told to come back Sunday morning for another trip into the red zone.

On the same Saturday afternoon, Buzz Smith and his sons sat around their crackling campfire eating dinner. Ten-year-old Eric and seven-year-old Adam were camping with their dad about eight miles from

A view of Mount St. Helens from the Coldwater II observation point on May 17, 1980.

Mount St. Helens. Twelve miles north of the mountain, Bruce Nelson, Sue Ruff, and four friends were also eating dinner. The group was tired after a day of hiking and about ready to crawl into their sleeping bags at the Green River campground.

Thirty miles due east of Mount St. Helens, twelve mountain climbers met to look over their equipment. They planned to scale Mount Adams the following day. They would meet at first light on Sunday morning to begin their climb up the 12,276-foot-tall mountain.

On the north side of Mount St. Helens, a crew of twenty-five United States Forest Service employees finished up their work on Saturday afternoon. They climbed into their trucks, tired and muddy after a day of planting trees. They had been working at the base of the mountain. They were scheduled to return Sunday morning to plant more trees on the south side of the peak.

Geologist David Johnston had traded shifts with a friend and was also scheduled to work on Sunday. Saturday afternoon he drove up to the Coldwater II observation point and got out of his Jeep. Johnston carried his supplies into a small trailer, which was perched on the edge of a ridge five miles from the volcano. A team of scientists took turns staying at the site to keep a close eye on the mountain and its growing bulge. A major eruption at Mount St. Helens seemed likely, but when?

RUMBLING IN THE EARTH

THE EARTH HAS EXPERIENCED many killer volcanoes during its long history. One of the most famous happened in Pompeii, Italy. When Mount Vesuvius erupted in 79 A.D., some people in the city ran, but others hid in their homes. Poisonous gases in the air killed all those who did not escape. A very heavy ash-fall then buried the town.

Pompeii remained hidden for centuries, until workers digging a canal found part of the town in 1594. Since that time, archaeologists have uncovered the entire city of Pompeii. Houses, clothing, furniture, and even food were preserved under the ash. The skeletons of many of Pompeii's residents also lay where they had fallen centuries ago.

The worst volcanic eruption in modern times happened on the island of Krakatoa, which is part of Indonesia. A huge eruption in 1883 created a tsunami more than one hundred feet high. The wall of water roared into the town of Anjer, sweeping away everything in its path. Houses, animals, and people were all carried away. More than thirty-five thousand people died as a result of the terrible flooding.

In this illustration, Pompeii residents run for cover as Mount Vesuvius erupts in 79 A.D. The ancient city remained buried for centuries until it was discovered in 1594.

Poisonous hot gas was responsible for killing thirty thousand people on the Caribbean island of Martinique. When Mount Pelée erupted in 1902, a cloud of toxic gases roared down the mountain at one hundred miles per hour. It reached the town of St. Pierre in two minutes. People had no time to escape the deadly gas. There were only a few survivors left in St. Pierre after the eruption. One of them was a convicted murderer who had been locked up in an underground dungeon.

Volcanoes are formed when molten rock, called magma, pushes up through vents, or weak spots, in the earth's crust. Magma, which is full of hot gases, creates great pressure under the earth's surface. When the ground can no longer hold back the intense pressure, there is an eruption. Magma, gas, steam, and ash spew out of the vent and into the air. Magma that reaches the earth's surface is called lava.

The earth's crust is made up of huge plates or sections that are many miles thick. Most volcanoes are located along the boundaries of these tectonic plates. According to United States Forest Service public affairs officer Tom Corcoran, "Much like pieces of a jigsaw puzzle, the earth's surface is broken into a number of shifting plates. There are probably 12 major plates and many smaller ones. These plates . . . drift either away from a neighboring plate or toward or past the next one."[1]

The plates shift and move constantly. Sometimes, the edge of one plate is gradually pushed underneath the edge of another one. The grinding together of these two huge landmasses creates friction, which melts the rocks and heats up the water and gases under the earth's crust. The molten rock and steam push up, looking for a place to escape.

Seventy-five percent of the active volcanoes found on land today are located in an area called the "Ring of Fire." This is an area surrounding the Pacific Ocean, where water meets land. There is a huge tectonic plate under the Pacific Ocean. Smaller plates lie under the land that surrounds the ocean. Many volcanoes are located where these shifting plates meet.

Mount St. Helens is part of a chain of mountains known as the Cascade Range. These mountains are part of the earth's Ring of Fire. The Cascades extend from British Columbia in Canada through the states of Washington, Oregon, and California. Thirteen of the

Most of Earth's volcanoes are located in the Ring of Fire. Many volcanoes are found where shifting tectonic plates meet.

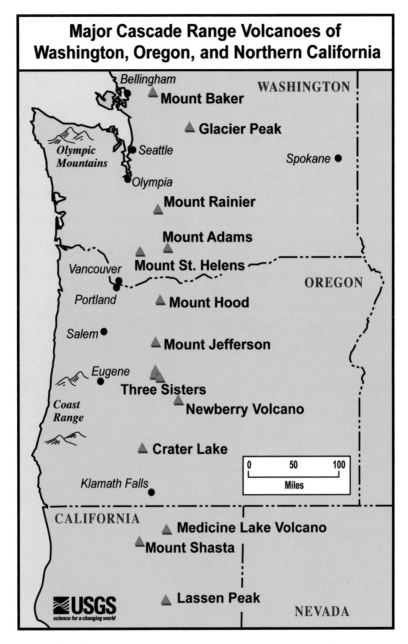

Major Cascade Range Volcanoes of Washington, Oregon, and Northern California

Bellingham

WASHINGTON

▲ Mount Baker

▲ Glacier Peak

Olympic
Mountains

● Seattle

Spokane ●

●Olympia

▲ Mount Rainier

▲ Mount Adams

Vancouver

▲ Mount St. Helens

OREGON

Portland

▲ Mount Hood

Salem ●

▲ Mount Jefferson

Eugene
●

▲ Three Sisters

Coast
Range

▲ Newberry Volcano

▲ Crater Lake

| 0 | 50 | 100 |

Miles

Klamath Falls
●

CALIFORNIA

▲ Medicine Lake Volcano

▲ Mount Shasta

USGS
science for a changing world

▲ Lassen Peak

NEVADA

Mount St. Helens is part of the Cascade mountain range, which extends from British Columbia in Canada down to California. This map shows the thirteen volcanic mountains in the Cascade Range.

mountains in the Cascade Range may be volcanic. They have erupted in the past and might do so again.

Mount St. Helens has erupted many times in the past. Peter Frenzen, a scientist who studies volcanoes, explained that "During the 4,000 years preceding 1980, Mount St. Helens erupted enough lava, pumice, and ash to build the entire mountain we see today."[2] Mount St. Helens is a composite volcano. This type of volcano is formed when material from deep inside the earth spills out or erupts. More and more layers are added with each eruption until a mountain is gradually built.

Mount St. Helens got its name from Captain George Vancouver, a member of the British Royal Navy. He was part of a crew that explored the Pacific coast in 1792. After seeing the beautiful mountain, Vancouver named it in honor of the British ambassador to Spain, Lord St. Helens.

Long before Captain Vancouver arrived in the area, American Indians gave the mountain many different names. Some called it Lawelatla, which means "one from whom smoke comes." Other Indians named the peak Loo-Wit for "keeper of the fires," or Tah-One-Lat-Clah, which means "fire mountain."[3]

In 1800, there was a major eruption on Mount St. Helens. It was described in diaries and letters by explorers and traders in the area. During the next fifty-seven years, settlers reported many smaller eruptions. Then, after 1857, the mountain seemed to settle down. It stayed quiet until 1980, when it came to life again.

CHAPTER THREE

"THIS IS IT!"

ON SUNDAY, MAY 18, 1980, David Johnston was ready for work as the sun began to shine on the Coldwater II observation site. It was a beautiful morning, so Johnston could see the mountain clearly from his position five miles away. He took several measurements of the bulge on the north face. Johnston also checked the seismograms to see if there had been any more earthquakes. Seismograms are the written records made by seismographs, machines that record the earth's vibrations.

Two other geologists, Keith and Dorothy Stoeffel, wanted to get a closer look at Mount St. Helens on Sunday morning. They flew in a small plane over the mountain so they could see down into the crater. Dorothy Stoeffel said, "We arrived at 7:50 in the restricted zone, and made two passes directly over the crater and several around the mountain . . . it didn't look like an active volcano—more like one going to sleep."[1]

Then Keith Stoeffel noticed some debris sliding down the mountain and started taking pictures. "Suddenly, the whole north half of the mountain began sliding away, directly beneath our feet," exclaimed Dorothy.[2] The pilot made a sharp turn and raced away for safety.

An aerial photograph of the Mount St. Helens eruption on May 18, 1980. Geologists Keith and Dorothy Stoeffel flew in a small plane over the volcano. Looking into the crater, it did not look like a volcano ready to erupt. The scientists did not know an earthquake had rocked the volcano, pushing it toward a fiery eruption.

The geologists flying above the volcano did not know it at the time, but an earthquake measuring 5.1 on the Richter scale had struck Mount St. Helens. The Richter scale is used to measure the strength of an earthquake. Violent tremors shook loose the huge bulge on the north face. Tons of the mountain's mass began sliding down its north face in a giant avalanche. With the weight and pressure of the bulge gone, gas and ash that had been trapped in the volcano's core exploded outward.

As the Stoeffels' plane was making its escape, the twelve climbers on Mount Adams noticed streaks of smoke above Mount St. Helens, thirty miles to their west. Fred Grimm described it as "a little puff, at the top of the mountain. Then, within two or three seconds, it appeared that the north side of the mountain just blew out."[3] The mountain climbers watched in horror as "the whole top of the mountain was engulfed in the column of smoke. It rose like an atomic explosion . . . with sort of a shock wave that went to the north."[4]

From his vantage point at the Coldwater II observation point just five miles from the volcano, David Johnston watched the mountain explode. At 8:32 A.M., he grabbed his two-way radio and yelled, "Vancouver, Vancouver, this is it!"[5] Then the radio went dead.

The explosion sent a cloud of superheated poisonous gases, steam, and debris blasting out of the mountain. The scalding cloud shot sideways to the north, roasting everything in its path. Huge trees were knocked down like so many toothpicks, their leaves stripped by winds moving at speeds as fast as three hundred miles per hour. Poisonous gases and ash filled the air, while rocks rained down.

While the main explosion blasted across the land, lighter ash and steam rose in an enormous plume from the volcano. Up and up it went, until the ash cloud was sixteen miles high. Winds in the upper atmosphere carried the ash over the countryside, where it later fell like hot, black snow.

On the south side of Mount St. Helens, the crew of twenty-five tree-planters were busy digging holes. Kran Kilpatrick said that when the eruption began on the other side of the mountain, "There was no sound to it, not a sound—it was like a silent movie, and we were all in it. First the ash cloud shot out to the east, then to the west, then some lighter stuff started shooting straight up. At the same time the ash

This photo of David Johnston was taken on May 17, 1980, the day before the volcanic eruption. Johnston, watching the mountain explode, said "Vancouver, Vancouver, this is it!" before his radio went dead.

curtain started coming right down the south slope toward us. I could see boulders—they must have been huge—being hurled out of the leading edge...."[6] The crew members ran for their six trucks and raced away to safety. The day before they had been working on the north side of the mountain, in an area that was blown away by the eruption.

Buzz Smith and his sons had just finished eating breakfast at their campsite that Sunday morning when they heard what sounded like three rifle shots. Then golf-ball-size stones began raining down on them, followed by what sounded like a "low-flying jet coming in on top of us."[7] Smith grabbed his sons and crawled under a fallen tree, pulling a sleeping bag over their heads. Wet ash from the eruption covered the bag and turned the sky black.

As hot ash and gases shot out of the volcano, the intense heat melted tons of ice and snow on the mountain. The liquid mixed with loose rocks and dirt to form raging rivers of mud. The mud joined with boiling lava that was gushing out of the crater. An avalanche of hot mud and lava roared down the sides of the mountain at speeds over one hundred miles per hour.

"One tongue of the avalanche slammed into Spirit Lake . . . causing the water level to rise nearly 200 feet as debris from the avalanche came to rest in the lake's bottom,"[8] said Tom Corcoran, the public affairs specialist for the United States Forest Service. "The bulk of the avalanche was deflected westward down the North Fork Toutle River, leaving behind a hummocky deposit more than 600 feet deep in some places."[9]

During the volcanic eruption on May 18, 1980, a plume of steam and ash rose sixteen miles into the air. It engulfed the countryside in darkness. The ash fell like hot, black snow.

Those still alive in the blast zone could only cover their heads and pray for the nightmare to stop. Buzz Smith knew he had to get his sons out of the area. When the ash-fall got a little lighter, the Smiths grabbed some extra clothing and began walking. They had to use a compass to guide their way because, blinded by smoke and ash, they could see only a few feet ahead. They covered their mouths and noses with the extra pieces of clothing, trying to keep the ash out of their lungs.

Ash clouds hover over the Ephrata airport in Washington a day after the eruption of Mount St. Helens. For the people who survived the initial volcanic explosion, they had to trek through suffocating ash, steam, and poisonous gas to reach safety. Hikers could not see more than a few feet in front of them.

Photographer David Crockett from Seattle's KOMO television station was struggling to stay alive, too. He had been taking pictures from a logging road near the base of Mount St. Helens when the eruption quickly engulfed him in a dark cloud. He said into his tape recorder, "I can hear the mountain rumble. . . . It's very, very hard to breathe and very dark. If I could only breathe air. God, just give me a breath."[10] The blowing, swirling ash created static electricity, which sent lightning bolts streaking through the sky. Forest fires set by lightning strikes added smoke to the already ash-filled air.

Hikers Bruce Nelson, Sue Ruff, and Terry Crall had been cooking breakfast at their campsite when the mountain blew. Ruff said, "We saw this thick yellow-and-black cloud rushing toward us. I remember thinking, 'I should take a picture of it.' Then I thought we'd better hide."[11] Crall ran to a tent to get Karen Varner. Nelson and Ruff held each other as trees fell around them and ash rained down. Before long, the pair was buried in ash. They could not breathe under all of the ash and had to get out. Nelson said, "Sue and I started digging our way out of the ash, which was so hot that it burned our hands. Our mouths were full of mud. I told Sue we were going to die, and she said, 'Nonsense.'"[12]

After Nelson and Ruff clawed their way out of the ash, their heads were pelted with stones falling from the sky. Gagging from the ash and gas fumes, they covered their mouths with sweatshirts and started looking for their friends. They found only two, Dan Balch and Brian Thomas. Both were barely alive and in shock. They could not possibly walk to safety, so Sue Ruff and Bruce Nelson set out to get help.

CHAPTER FOUR

HELP ARRIVES

FAMILY MEMBERS WERE WORRIED about their missing relatives. They frantically called the United States Forest Service and the Washington state police. Where were their loved ones? Had they survived the horrible eruption? More than two hundred people were unaccounted for immediately after the blast.

As soon as the ash had cleared enough on Sunday afternoon to restore some visibility, military helicopters were sent into the blast zone. They looked for survivors. The searchers flew low, trying to find anything that moved. People stranded since morning waved desperately at the helicopters as they passed overhead. Some were caught in areas flooded by rising river water. Others were slogging through the ash, lost in the once beautiful forest. Rescue crews evacuated dozens of people.

Buzz Smith and his sons had been walking for hours. They did not know it yet, but they had been the closest people to the explosion to survive. Buzz Smith said that as they walked, "I saw deer with their eyes

1979

1981

The 1980 eruption completely destroyed the forest surrounding the volcano. The top photo shows flourishing vegetation before the eruption, and the bottom photo shows the wasteland the forest became after it.

burned out and their fur smoking. Birds were lying on the ground. I kept thinking, 'This has got to be as close to hell on earth as I'll ever see.'"[1]

While they were stumbling through the ash on Sunday afternoon, the Smith family met a man who was badly burned. The injured man joined the Smiths on their journey to safety. Breathing ash all day had caused them to become extremely thirsty. Smith and his sons dug through the ash and found clean spring water. They all knelt down to drink the wonderful, cooling liquid before resuming their desperate walk to safety.

Finally, late on Sunday afternoon, the sound of a helicopter filled the air. As the Smiths waved their clothing in the air and yelled, hoping to attract attention, the helicopter circled and landed near the exhausted survivors. At 7:50 P.M., eleven hours after the eruption of Mount St. Helens began, Buzz, Adam, and Eric Smith were finally rescued. The burned man was taken aboard the helicopter, too. He was flown to a hospital and eventually recovered from his injuries.

Bruce Nelson and Sue Ruff had also walked through a desert of ash. Along the way, a sixty-year-old man joined them. The three exhausted people sang songs to help keep themselves going. They had been walking for hours when they heard the sound of a helicopter. They quickly grabbed pieces of clothing and began beating the dust and ash at their feet to create a huge dust cloud. The helicopter crew saw the cloud and swooped down to pick up the survivors.

After they were picked up, Bruce Nelson and Sue Ruff were able to guide the helicopter pilot back to their campsite. They found their friends Brian Thomas and Dan Balch still alive when the aircraft touched down. The badly injured men were brought aboard and flown to a hospital, where they later recovered. The bodies of their other friends, Karen Varner and Terry Crall, were later found at the campsite by searchers.

A Washington National Guard helicopter pilot surveys downed trees and mudslides in search of survivors after the eruption. It was difficult for the search-and-rescuers to see because of the dark ash.

David Crockett was one of the lucky ones who managed to survive his ordeal. The twenty-eight-year-old news photographer had been walking since morning when a helicopter crew spotted him Sunday afternoon. When the pilot landed, the thankful Crockett ran toward the rescue aircraft and climbed aboard. He was still carrying his camera and tape recorder.

A car is completely submerged in ash on May 20, 1980, after Mount St. Helens erupted. *National Geographic* photographer Reid Blackburn was found dead in his car after it had been buried up to the windows in ash.

Another photographer, Reid Blackburn, was not as fortunate. He had been taking pictures for *National Geographic* magazine and the United States Geological Service when Mount St. Helens erupted. His body was later found by searchers. He was still in his car, which was buried up to the windows in ash.

Geologist David Johnston also lost his life on May 18, 1980. From his observation point on Coldwater Ridge, Johnston took the full impact of the blast. After his final message to Vancouver, he was never heard from again. When helicopters flew over his campsite, everything was gone. The trailer, Jeep, and all of the equipment had been blown away. In their place were broken tree trunks and huge boulders covered with ash. In spite of several searches, David Johnston's body was never found.

Harry Truman suffered a similar fate. He died in his beloved lodge on Spirit Lake, along with his sixteen cats. When searchers flew over the site, they saw that the lodge had been buried under hundreds of feet of ash and debris.

Some of the volcano's victims had been buried in mud and ash. Others suffocated or were burned to death by the searing hot poisonous gases. Fifty-seven people lost their lives during the eruption of Mount St. Helens on May 18, 1980. Many of the bodies were never found. The ones that were found were taken to the Toledo, Washington, airport. The U.S. Army had set up a tent there to use as a temporary morgue.

AFTERMATH

ONCE THE MISSING AND DEAD were accounted for, officials looked at other damages caused by the eruption. The five- or six-mile area north of the mountain looked like the site of an atomic bomb blast. Gray mud and ash covered the landscape. Gone were millions of towering trees, animals, and plants. In their place was a gray, sterile world. Nothing that was above the ground in this area survived the eruption.

Mud and lava flowing from the volcano had done a great deal of damage. The mudflows carried along blocks of ice, trees, pieces of houses, and burning wood. Debris poured into area waterways, crushing bridges and flooding roads. The rivers of mud were so powerful that they even picked up train cars and swept them away.

As hot mud filled the local rivers, temperatures in the water rose dramatically. The water in the North Fork Toutle River, usually around 50 degrees Fahrenheit, rose to 90 degrees. Fish leaped out of the steamy water onto the banks. An estimated 70 million trout and salmon were killed by the mudflows.

A logger walks across a huge tree felled during the eruption. Millions of trees were stripped of their leaves and toppled over, all pointing in the same direction.

Farther from the blast, trees were toppled and stripped of their leaves. All of the fallen trees pointed in the same direction—away from the blast. The hills north of Mount St. Helens seemed to be covered with piles of huge toothpicks. Would life ever return to this devastated land? About one hundred and fifty thousand acres had been damaged or destroyed by the volcanic eruption. When President Jimmy Carter flew over the area he said, "I've never seen anything like it. The moon looks like a golf course compared to what's up there."[1]

Ash was a terrible problem following the eruption. For nine hours, Mount St. Helens spewed ash fifteen miles up into the atmosphere. Millions of tons of ash filled the air. Eventually, it all came down, burying roadways and towns. Winds carried the ash in an easterly and northeasterly direction. Cities in the path, such as Yakima, Washington, Missoula, Montana, and Moscow, Idaho, had heavy ash deposits. Lighter amounts of ash fell as far away as Wyoming, Colorado, Nebraska, and South Dakota. The finest ash particles were caught in the winds of the upper atmosphere and circled the earth many times.

Falling ash clogged air filters in the engines of cars, trucks, trains, and airplanes. Transportation came to a halt in the areas most heavily hit by the ash cloud. The ash also made breathing difficult and burned people's eyes. A Missoula, Montana, resident said, "I feel like someone popped my eyeballs out and rolled them around in a sandbox."[2]

One of the hardest hit cities was Yakima, Washington, eighty miles northeast of Mount St. Helens. By noon on the day of the eruption, Yakima was plunged into darkness. Streetlights went on as if night

This farmer sprays a cherry orchard that is covered in ash on May 21, 1980, after the eruption of Mount St. Helens. Falling ash was a huge problem in the areas surrounding the volcano. However, ash also fell as far away as Wyoming, Colorado, Nebraska, and South Dakota.

In this photo, two Yakima, Washington, residents walk down the dark, ash-covered streets at 3:00 P.M. on the day of the eruption. Although it was mid-afternoon, it looked like the middle of the night.

The clean up of the city was a massive job, and more than six hundred thousand tons of ash were hauled out of Yakima. These two men shovel ash into the back of a pickup truck on May 21, 1980.

had fallen. Ash filled the streets and seeped into closed windows. The town's water treatment plant was clogged with ash. Schools and businesses were shut down. The heavy ash flattened hayfields surrounding the town.

Residents in Yakima wore facemasks as they tried to clean up the tons of ash that blanketed the city. Spraying water on the mess only made the situation worse. When the ash mixed with water, it turned into cement. The mountains of ash had to be collected in bags and hauled away. Yakima Mayor Betty Edmondson said, "Things aren't going to be normal for quite awhile."[3] It took Yakima a month to clean up the ash and grit covering the town.

As residents of affected towns bagged the ash, National Guard trucks were there to collect it. In Yakima alone, six hundred thousand tons of ash were hauled away. It is estimated that 540 million tons of ash fell on more than twenty-two thousand square miles of Earth.

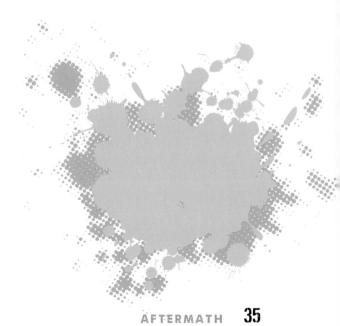

CHAPTER SIX

THE FUTURE

BEFORE THE 1980 ERUPTION, Mount St. Helens was 9,677 feet tall. It was a beautiful snowcapped mountain, full of forests and wildlife. Birds soared in the clear air around the peak, while deer and elk nibbled on green grass and plants on the mountain's flanks. Squirrels ran from tree to tree and insects buzzed in the cold, clear air. Occasionally, bears could be seen catching fish in a rushing stream. During springtime, wildflowers such as lupine and fireweed covered the slopes of Mount St. Helens. The area attracted hikers and campers because of its natural beauty and abundant wildlife.

All of that changed on May 18. Within a minute, thirteen hundred feet of the mountain were pulverized and blown away. In the hardest-hit blast zone right around Mount St. Helens, it would seem that nothing could have survived the intense heat. Surprisingly, however, many living things did survive the eruption.

Many seeds and roots were not destroyed because they were underground, protected by a layer of dirt or snow. Some small animals such as mice, gophers, and squirrels also survived in their underground burrows. As these creatures dug holes and tunnels, they pushed soil up to the surface. Seeds lodged in the soil and took root. Large colonies of ants also survived in their elaborate dirt cities, as did snakes hibernating in holes.

Although the natural landscape surrounding Mount St. Helens was devastated by the 1980 eruption, some living things did survive. Seeds, roots, and burrowing animals survived. In this photo, grass grows in a bed of moss near a stream about five miles from the volcano on April 22, 2010.

By the spring of 1981, small green shoots began appearing in some areas around Mount St. Helens. Fireweed, with its dark red blossoms, grew up through the cracked soil. Ants crawled over dead tree trunks. Gradually, birds returned to the area, along with flying insects. Spiders spun webs among the broken branches of the destroyed trees. Slowly, the waters of area lakes began to sparkle again.

In 1982, the United States Congress created the Mount St. Helens National Volcanic Monument. This monument is not a building or statue, but a 110,000-acre tract of land that was damaged or destroyed by the volcano. Inside the tract, nature is being allowed to do its repair work without any help. Trees that were blown down in the eruption still lie where they fell. Boulders that were thrown from the mountain remain where they landed on May 18, 1980. The monument is a living laboratory where scientists and visitors can learn how the land repairs itself after a volcanic eruption.

Visitors also come to the National Volcanic Monument just to see the mountain. Even though it is not as beautiful as it once was, Mount St. Helens is still an impressive sight. Thirteen thousand permits a year are issued to those who want to climb the mountain. Hikers cannot go into the crater, but they can stand on the rim and look at the growing lava dome. Many other hiking trails and campgrounds are also open to monument visitors.

There are three visitor centers near Mount St. Helens. At the Mount St. Helens Visitor Center, exhibits and a movie help explain what led to the May 18, 1980, eruption. The Coldwater Ridge center has videos

An elk stretches along a ridge about five miles from the volcano on November 17, 2004. In 1982, the U.S. Congress created the Mount St. Helens National Volcanic Monument. This monument allows the 110,000-acre tract of land that was damaged or destroyed during the 1980 eruption to repair itself without any human interference.

and displays showing how plants and animals have returned to the blast zone. From this site, visitors can also see the volcano and the Toutle River Valley, which was filled with debris from the May 18 landslides.

The Johnston Ridge Observatory was named in memory of David Johnston, the geologist who died during the eruption. It is built very close to the Coldwater II site where Johnston worked. From the outdoor deck just five miles from the mountain, visitors get a breathtaking view of the crater, the blast zone, and landslide deposits. Inside the building, exhibits describe the events that led to the eruption. Methods currently being used to monitor the mountain for volcanic activity are also explained in various displays.

Scientists continue to keep a close watch on the mountain. They do not want to be caught off guard like they were in 1980. Even though the 1980 eruption was expected, it was much stronger and happened sooner than anyone had predicted. Seismographs are still used to detect any earthquakes. Gases coming from the volcano are also measured. A change in the level and type of gas emissions could mean the mountain is heating up again.

Scientists are using a newer monitoring method to keep track of Mount St. Helens: the Global Positioning System. GPS uses orbiting satellites to pinpoint locations on Earth. GPS is being used to measure changes on the mountain's surface. University of Miami professor Timothy Dixon explains, "GPS offers us a three-dimensional picture of changes on the exterior of the volcano. In turn, these changes are related to the pressure that is being built up within the magma chamber."[1]

Since the 1980 disaster, there have been dozens of smaller eruptions on Mount St. Helens. United States Geological Survey geologist Ed Klimasauskas reported, "Since the last eruption, magma beneath the lava dome has continued to cool, crystallize, and solidify. As this happens, gases trapped in the molten rock are forced out. Pockets of gas build up pressure and eventually cause the surrounding rock to break, resulting in small earthquakes."[2]

Visitors walk near Mount St. Helens at the Johnston Ridge Observatory on May 18, 2010, the thirtieth anniversary of the 1980 eruption. This beautiful observatory is named after geologist David Johnston, who died during the eruption.

In this photo, the crater and the lava dome of Mount St. Helens is seen from the Johnston Ridge Observatory on May 14, 2010. In February 2011, an earthquake struck the volcano, causing steam to puff out of the crater. The volcano rumbles from time to time, but when will the next eruption happen?

Normally, about sixty small earthquakes are detected each month at Mount St. Helens. But in June 1998, there were 318 earthquakes. That number rose to 445 in July 1998. "Although this past year's seismic swarm did not result in an eruption, Mount St. Helens has given us notice that she is warming up for the next millennium . . . and the next eruption!" said Klimasauskas in 1999.[3]

After the activity in 1998, the mountain settled down until 2004. During September of that year, there was an increase in the number of earthquakes. At times, there were as many as four earthquakes per minute. The alert level was raised and the mountain was closed to climbers. In October 2004, several plumes of steam and ash shot into the air.

In March 2005, a plume of steam and ash shot 36,000 feet into the air. That is as high as most airliners cruise. The mountain was building a new lava dome that could be seen from the Johnston Ridge Observatory. The new dome was as big as a football field.

February 2011 saw the second biggest earthquake since Mount St. Helens erupted in 1980. Since that time, it has rumbled and puffed steam into the air daily. Is the mountain getting ready to blow again?

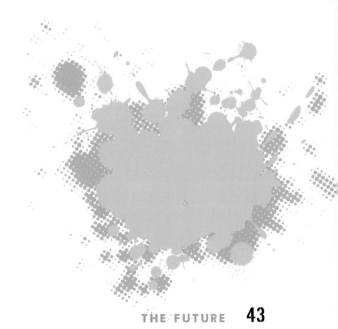

CHAPTER NOTES

CHAPTER 1. THE GIANT ROARS

1. Rowe Findley, "St. Helens: Mountain With a Death Wish," *National Geographic,* January 1981, p. 22.
2. Ibid., p. 16.

CHAPTER 2. RUMBLING IN THE EARTH

1. Tom Corcoran, *Mount St. Helens: The Story Behind the Scenery* (Las Vegas, Nev.: KC Publications, 1985), p. 20.
2. Peter Frenzen, "Nineteen Years Later Forest Rebirth is Well Underway," *Volcano Review*, Summer/Fall 1991, p. 8.
3. Corcoran, p. 40.

CHAPTER 3. "THIS IS IT!"

1. Rowe Findley, "St. Helens: In the Path of Destruction," *National Geographic*, January 1981, p. 42.
2. Ibid.
3. David Alpern, "The Convulsion of St. Helens," *Newsweek*, June 2, 1980, p. 22.
4. Ibid.
5. Jack McClintock, "Under the Volcano," *Discover*, November 1999, p. 88.
6. Findley, p. 43.
7. Maria Wilhelm, "Five Years Later, Nature and Man Rise Phoenix-Like From the Ashes of Mount St. Helens," *People*, May 20, 1985, p. 116.
8. Tom Corcoran, *Mount St. Helens: The Story Behind the Scenery* (Las Vegas, Nev.: KC Publications, 1985), p. 9.
9. Ibid.
10. "God, I Want to Live," *Time*, June 2, 1980, p. 26.
11. Ibid., p. 30.
12. Ibid.

CHAPTER 4. HELP ARRIVES

1. Maria Wilhelm, "Five Years Later, Nature and Man Rise Phoenix-Like From the Ashes of Mount St. Helens," *People*, May 20, 1985, p. 116.

CHAPTER 5. AFTERMATH

1. David Alpern, "The Convulsion of St. Helens," *Newsweek*, June 2, 1980, p. 23.

2. "God, I Want to Live," *Time*, June 2, 1980, p. 31.

3. Alpern, p. 28.

CHAPTER 6. THE FUTURE

1. Siobhan McCready, "Volcanoes Inside and Out," *Sea Frontiers*, October 1994, p. 3.

2. Ed Kilmasauskas, "Mount St. Helens Prepares to Rumble Into the New Millennium," *Volcano Review*, Spring/Summer 1999, p. 9.

3. Ibid.

GLOSSARY

avalanche—A mass of snow, earth, or rocks that suddenly slides down a mountain.

crater—A bowl-shaped cavity.

dormant—Quiet, as if asleep.

earthquake—A shaking of the crust of the earth.

Earth's crust—The outer layer of the earth.

friction—The rubbing of one object against another.

geologist—A scientist who studies the composition of the earth.

lava—Magma that pours out of a volcano.

magma—Molten rock found under the earth's crust.

pumice—Lightweight volcanic rock.

seismograph—An instrument that measures and records the motion of an earthquake.

tectonic plate—A large section of the earth's crust.

vent—A split or opening in the earth's crust.

volcano—An eruption of magma, gas, and ash through a vent in the earth's crust.

FURTHER READING

BOOKS

Ganeri, Anita. *Volcanoes in Action*. New York: Rosen Publishing Group, 2009.

Halpern, Monica. *Rivers of Fire: The Story of Volcanoes*. Washington, D.C.: National Geographic, 2006.

Harper, Kristine. *The Mount St. Helens Volcanic Eruptions*. New York: Facts on File, 2005.

O'Shei, Tim. *Volcanic Eruption!: Susan Ruff and Bruce Nelson's Story of Survival*. Mankato, Minn.: Capstone Press, 2007.

Riley, Gail Blasser. *Volcano!: The 1980 Mount St. Helens Eruption*. New York: Bearport Publishing, 2006.

INTERNET ADDRESSES

Mount St. Helens National Volcanic Monument
<www.fs.usda.gov/mountsthelens/>

Mount St. Helens.com
<http://mountsthelens.com/>

National Geographic: Volcanoes
<http://www.nationalgeographic.com/eye/volcanoes/volcanoes.html>

INDEX